What's in this book

This book belongs to

_____

换牙了 The wobbly tooth

学习内容 Contents

沟通 Communication

数一至十
Count from one to ten

介绍年龄
Talk about one's age

生词 New words

★	一	one	★ 八	eight
★	二	two	★ 九	nine
★	三	three	★ 十	ten
★	四	four	十二	twelve
★	五	five	岁	year of age
★	六	six	牙	tooth
★	七	seven		

句式 Sentence patterns

六岁，我开始换牙。

I will begin to lose my milk teeth when I am six years old.

跨学科学习 Project

制作牙齿模型，温习数字

Make a dental model and revise the numbers

文化 Cultures

世界各地换牙习俗

Tooth traditions from around the world

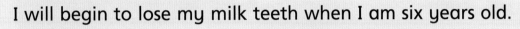

Get ready

1 How many teeth do you have now?

2 When did you lose your first tooth?

3 Have you ever met the tooth fairy?

liù suì
六岁

六岁，我开始换牙。

一颗牙，两颗牙。

七岁

sān
三

sì
四

三颗牙，四颗牙。

十岁 (shí suì)

五 (wǔ)

六 (liù)

七 (qī)

八 (bā)

五颗、六颗、七颗、
八颗……

jiǔ

九

shí

十

九颗牙，十颗牙。

十二岁，我有二十颗
新牙。

（图上文字）

shí èr suì
十二岁

Let's think

1 How many upper teeth of yours have fallen out so far?
Colour the teeth to show when they fell out.

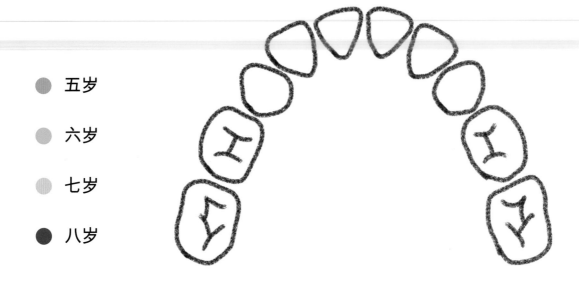

- 🔵 五岁
- 🔵 六岁
- 🔵 七岁
- ⚫ 八岁

2 How do we keep our teeth healthy? Tick the correct ways.

a

b

c

d

New words

1 Learn the new words.

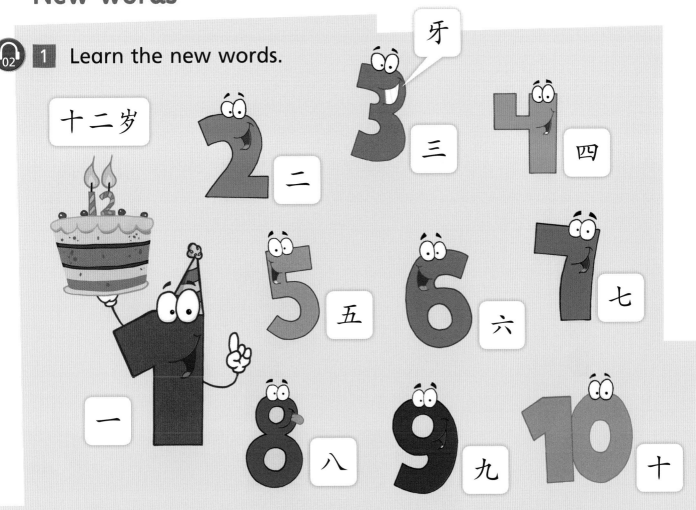

十二岁

2 二

3 三 牙

4 四

1 一

5 五

6 六

7 七

8 八

9 九

10 十

2 Join the numbers from one to ten and colour the picture.

听听说说 Listen and say

03 **1** Listen and match the keys to the correct doors.

04 **2** Look at the pictures. Listen to the sto[...]

1

2

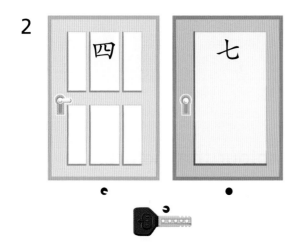

3

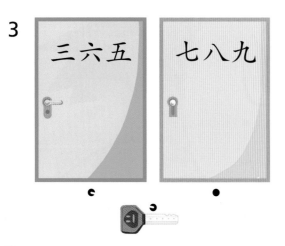

① 你好！你叫什么名字？

我叫丁浩。

③ 六、七、八、九、十……

你好！

...nd say.

一、二、三、四、五……

3 Tell your friend your phone number.

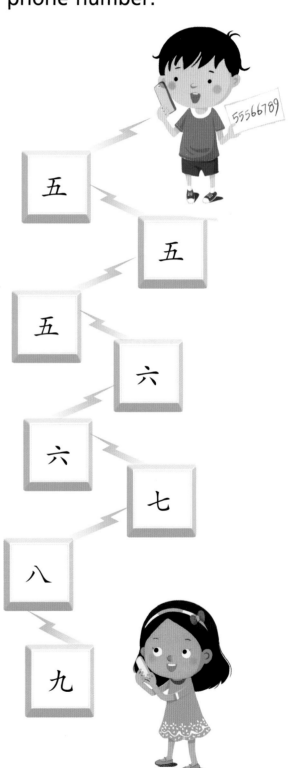

55566789

五
五
五
六
六
七
八
九

④ 谢谢！再见！

Task

Count the following items in your classroom. Write the numbers and say them in Chinese.

Game

Play with your friend. Read the numbers to create a path from 'Start' to 'Finish' and ask the other to draw it.

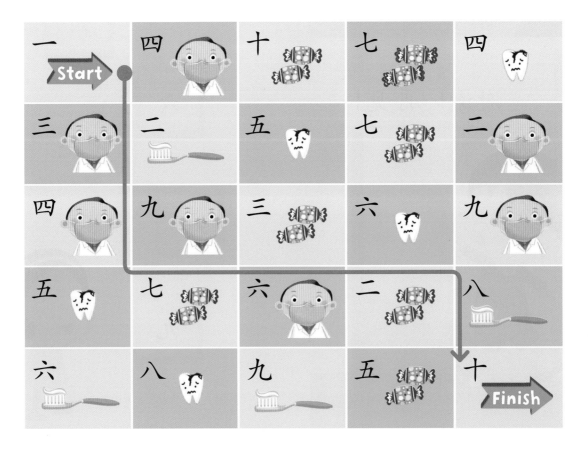

Song

🎧 05 **Listen and sing.**

一二三，三二一，
一二三四五六七，
八九十，十九八，
我有十颗小牙齿。

课堂用语 Classroom language

上学。
Go to school.

上课。
Class begins.

下课。
Class is over.

写一写 Write

1 Learn and trace the stroke.

捺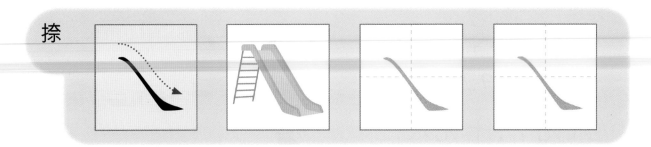

2 Learn the component. Circle 八 in the characters.

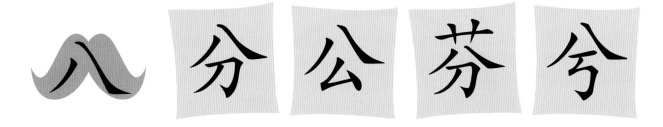

3 How many 八 can you find in the Chinese garden? Circle them.

4 Trace and write the character.

八 八

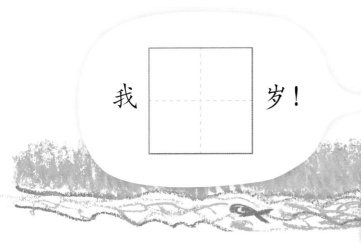

5 Write and say.

我 [ ] 岁！

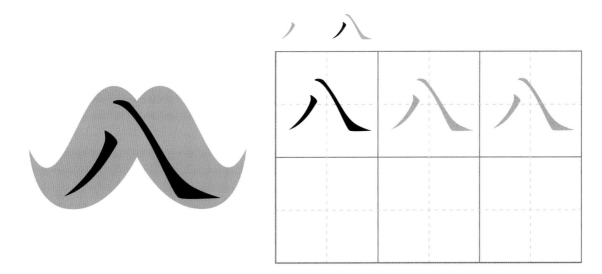

汉字小常识 Did you know?

Read the characters.

Some characters are made up of only one component.

一 八 人 五 女

Cultures

Find out what children around the world do when they lose their teeth. Write the letters.

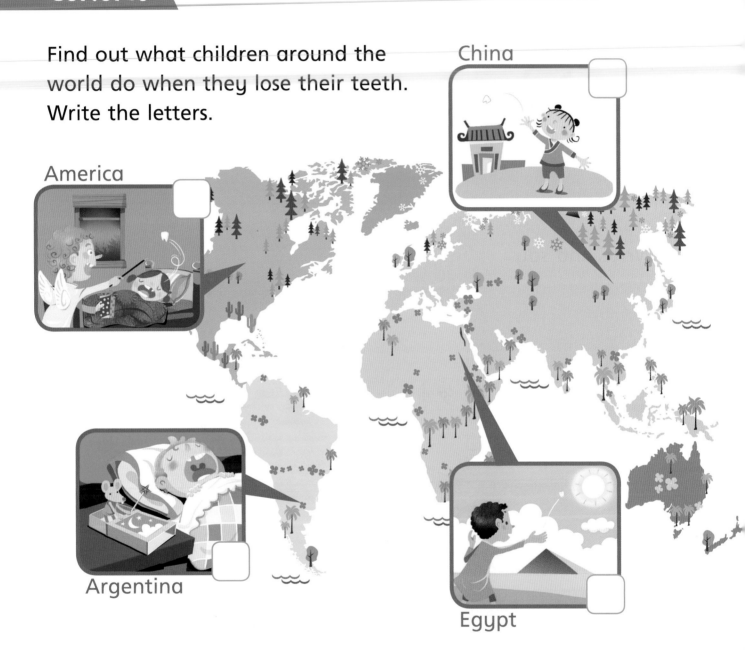

America

China

Argentina

Egypt

a	b	c	d
I throw my tooth towards the sun and the sun will send me a better one.	I put my tooth in a box. The tooth mouse will take it and leave me some money.	I place my upper tooth under the bed and my lower tooth on the roof. This way, my new teeth will grow healthily.	I put my tooth under my pillow. The tooth fairy will take it and give me a present.

Project

1 Make a dental model. Learn to clean your teeth the right way.

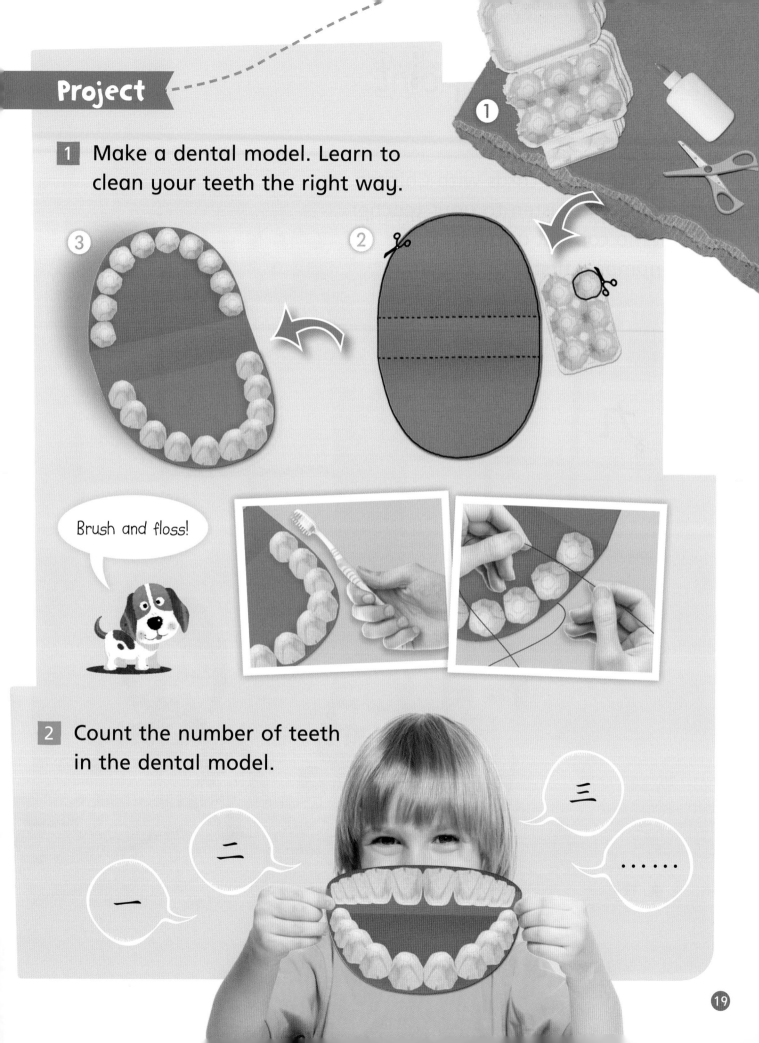

Brush and floss!

2 Count the number of teeth in the dental model.

一

二

三

......

1 Make bingo cards with Chinese numbers. Listen to your teacher. Who can get a row of three numbers first?

BINGO

九		
五	四	

2 Work with your friend. Colour the stars and the chillies.

Words	说	读	写
一	☆	☆	☆
二	☆	☆	☆
三	☆	☆	☆
四	☆	☆	🌶
五	☆	☆	🌶
六	☆	☆	☆
七	☆	☆	🌶
八	☆	☆	☆
九	☆	☆	🌶
十	☆	☆	☆

Words and sentences	说	读	写
十二	☆	☆	☆
岁	☆	🌶	🌶
牙	☆	🌶	🌶
我六岁。	☆	🌶	🌶

Count from one to ten	☆
Talk about one's age	☆

3 What does your teacher say?

My teacher says …

分享 Sharing

Words I remember

一	yī	one
二	èr	two
三	sān	three
四	sì	four
五	wǔ	five
六	liù	six
七	qī	seven
八	bā	eight
九	jiǔ	nine
十	shí	ten
十二	shí èr	twelve

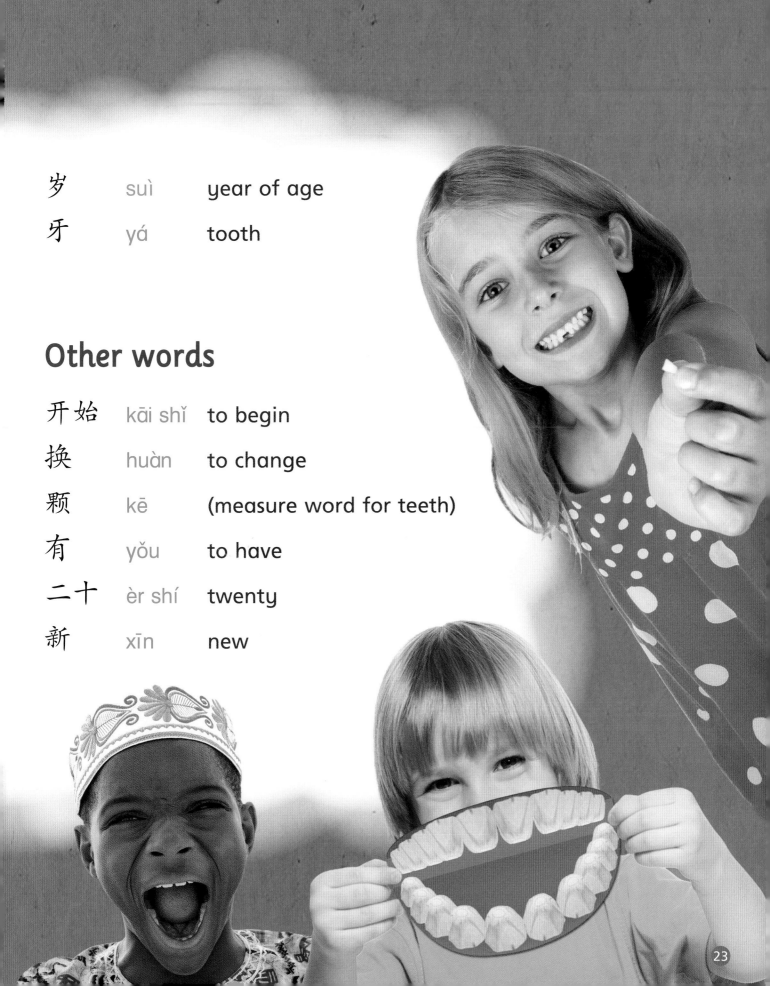

| 岁 | suì | year of age |
| 牙 | yá | tooth |

Other words

开始	kāi shǐ	to begin
换	huàn	to change
颗	kē	(measure word for teeth)
有	yǒu	to have
二十	èr shí	twenty
新	xīn	new

OXFORD
UNIVERSITY PRESS

Oxford University Press is a department of the University of Oxford.
It furthers the University's objective of excellence in research, scholarship,
and education by publishing worldwide. Oxford is a registered trade mark of
Oxford University Press in the UK and in certain other countries

Published in Hong Kong by
Oxford University Press (China) Limited
39th Floor, One Kowloon, 1 Wang Yuen Street, Kowloon Bay,
Hong Kong

Illustrated by Anne Lee and Wildman

Photographs for reproduction permitted by Dreamstime.com

China National Publications Import & Export (Group) Corporation is an authorized distributor of
Oxford Elementary Chinese.

Please contact content@cnpiec.com.cn or 86-10-65856782

ISBN: 978-0-19-942970-7

10 9 8 7 6 5 4 3 2